Davidson's three-wheeled 6 horsepower Duryea was converted into a quadricycle in 1899. It could transport four men and five thousand rounds of ammunition. The only armour was the bullet-proof shield over the Colt machine-gun.

EARLY ARMOURED CARS

E. Bartholomew

Shire Publications Ltd

CONTENTS

Set in 9 point Times roman and printed in Great Britain by C. I. Thomas & Sons (Haverfordwest) Ltd, Press Buildings, Merlins Bridge, Haverfordwest, Dyfed.

British Library Cataloguing in Publication Data available.

ACKNOWLEDGEMENTS
I would like to thank all my colleagues at the Tank Museum for their assistance, particularly the Curator, George Forty, the Librarian, David Fletcher, and the Photographer, Roland Groom. All photographs, including the cover illustration, are from the archives of the Tank Museum.

COVER: *One of the most successful armoured cars of the First World War was based on the 40/50 horsepower Rolls-Royce Silver Ghost chassis. This 1920-pattern vehicle has a revised turret and engine but is essentially the same as the model introduced in December 1914. Still in working order, it served across the globe during the inter-war years and is now on display at the Tank Museum, Bovington.*

One of the Fowler B5 armoured traction engines hauling a 6 inch (150 mm) howitzer into a wagon. The Fowlers could pull two field guns and three infantry-carrying wagons. They were armoured, with plates up to 6 mm (0.24 inch) thick, by Charles Cammell and Company Limited.

Frederick Simms with his 'Motor Scout' at its first public demonstration in Richmond Park in June 1899. The 1.5 horsepower de Dion quadricycle was unarmoured except for a shield. It was superseded by better protected and more powerful vehicles but was the forerunner of motorcycle and sidecar combinations used by British units during the First World War.

THE FIRST ARMOURED VEHICLES

When Nicholas-Joseph Cugnot invented the first mechanically propelled vehicle, he soon realised that it had a military application and offered his steam road carriage of 1769 to the French Army for use as an artillery tractor. His *'voiture à feu'* was turned down after trials, but during the course of the nineteenth century steam tractors were increasingly used for military transport and also featured in plans for the first armoured vehicles. In Britain, in 1855, James Cowen's projected steam 'Battle Car' was dismissed as barbaric, but in the American Civil War (1861-5) Charles S. Dickinson built a cannon-armed steam tractor for the Confederate Army, although it was not used in action. In 1900, during the Boer War, the British Army sent armoured Fowler steam tractors to South Africa to protect supply columns from raiders.

Steam tractors were too large and cumbersome to make effective fighting vehicles and the invention of the petrol engine provided a better, and relatively cheap, source of power. In 1896 an American inventor, E. J. Pennington, produced sketches of a petrol-engined armoured car which aroused considerable interest and publicity. Two years later another American, Major (later Colonel) Royal P. Davidson, fitted a three-wheeled Duryea car with a Colt machine-gun, although the only protection was an armoured shield. In Britain, during the same year, Frederick R. Simms produced a similar vehicle by fitting a Maxim machine-gun and bullet-proof shield to a 1.5 horsepower de Dion quadricycle. This 'Motor Scout' could hardly be called an armoured car, as it offered virtually no cover for the driver, so Simms developed a more sophisticated vehicle, which was

ABOVE: *Simms leans against the pom-pom on his Motor War Scout. The car had a crew of four but was also intended for use as a personnel carrier and could transport twelve infantrymen.*

BELOW: *The chain-driven Charron, Girardot et Voigt of 1902 had a Hotchkiss machine-gun mounted on a central pivot. The gunners were safeguarded by a 7 mm (0.28 inch) thick armoured compartment and shield, but there was no cover for the driver and front-seat passenger.*

For many years armoured car designers used the basic layout established by the 1904 Charron, Girardot et Voigt. This prototype was tested by the French Army and similar models with 35 horsepower engines were sold to Russia. In 1909 the German Army 'borrowed' two of the armoured cars which were en route across Europe and used them in their annual manoeuvres.

built by Vickers Sons and Maxim Limited. The fate of this 'Motor War Car', which ran on railway tracks, is not known, but in 1902 Simms demonstrated a similar road vehicle in a motor show at Crystal Palace. It closely resembled Pennington's design of six years earlier and was open-topped and shaped a little like an upturned boat. It was armed with a quick-firing Maxim 1 pdr 'pom-pom' and two machine-guns. The armoured hull was 6 mm (0.24 inch) thick and enclosed a 16 horsepower engine which ran on either petrol or oil and gave a top speed of about 10 mph (16 km/h). It was the first true armoured car and attracted large crowds to the exhibition but no orders from the War Office.

The military showed more interest in armoured cars in France, where a vehicle designed by the firm of Charron, Girardot et Voigt (CGV) was exhibited at a Paris motor show in 1902. The 40 horsepower car had an 8 mm Hotchkiss

machine-gun mounted in an armoured tub at the rear, but the driver and passenger were left in the open. It was tested by the French Army in 1902 and, although no further models of this type were built, CGV went on to produce the first fully enclosed armoured car, with a machine-gun mounted in a revolving turret. The car weighed about 3 tons, was powered by a 30 horsepower engine and had a top speed of 28 mph (45 km/h). It had self-sealing tyres to minimise damage from shrapnel and bullets and carried steel channels which could be laid across trenches. Two prototypes were built and one tested by the Ministry of War in February 1906 gave a good performance, although fumes from the gun made conditions inside very uncomfortable. The test car was then sent to French Morocco and the other was sold to the Russian government, which ordered a further ten, slightly improved vehicles. In 1909 Hotchkiss produced four armoured cars for the

Captain Genty at the wheel of his 24 horsepower Panhard et Levassor in 1904. Armed with its tripod-mounted machine-gun it had two of the essential features of an armoured fighting vehicle — firepower and mobility — but the third, protection, was non-existent.

Turkish Army. These resembled the original CGV of 1902 but were based on more advanced touring cars.

The export designs were better fighting vehicles than the French Army cars. Between 1904 and 1911 Captain Genty, a motoring enthusiast, armed several Panhards and Clement Bayards with machine-guns and the cars were used on trials in France and on patrols in Morocco, but fully armoured cars were not adopted by the French Army until 1914.

Most early military vehicles could travel only on roads or good ground so, in 1904, in Austria, Paul Daimler supervised the construction of a four-wheel-drive armoured car. The Austro-Daimler gave all-round protection to its three-man crew and had a Maxim machine-gun in a fully rotating turret. With armour 3 mm (0.12 inch) thick, it weighed 3 tons and the four cylinder, 35 horsepower engine gave a road speed of about 28 mph (45 km/h). The car was used in 1905 on German Army manoeuvres and a year later by the Austro-Hungarian Army. In

a demonstration before the Emperor Franz Josef, however, frightened horses bolted at the sound of the car's engine and imperial disapproval led to the abandonment of a profitable order.

In 1906 Austria's German allies used a lightly armoured Opel Darracq staff car on exercises. The German Army, however, was more concerned with countering the threat from the air, so in the same year Ehrhardt built a *Ballon Abwehrkanone* based on a 50/60 horsepower lorry chassis. It had a completely enclosed armoured body and a small, fixed turret that allowed its 50 mm gun to be used against ground targets. The Ehrhardt was followed by a series of anti-aircraft lorries, some of which were armoured. They were used by the Germans and the Austrians, but high-ranking officers had little enthusiasm for armoured vehicles and when war began in 1914 both armies were led into action by cavalry.

In the United States, Davidson continued his experiments in motorised

ABOVE: *The 1904 Austro-Daimler was the first four-wheel-drive armoured car. It was manufactured at Daimler's factory in Weiner-Neustadt. The car was modified a year after its construction when the rear of the dome-shaped turret was cut away. This gave room for an extra Maxim machine-gun, although one mount was left empty when this photograph was taken in 1906.*

RIGHT: *The 1906 Ehrhardt with its gun at maximum elevation. The turret could not be traversed, and this would have limited its effectiveness in combat.*

In 1902 Colonel Davidson's students at the Northwestern Military Academy built these two steam cars which were fitted with .30 Colt machine-guns. The cars were unreliable because of the difficulty of maintaining pressure in the boilers, so in 1909 Davidson turned once more to petrol-engined vehicles.

warfare. In 1902 he produced two steam cars and by 1903 had convinced the US Army Chief of Staff that cavalry regiments needed motor cars for reconnaissance. Although this far-sighted proposal was not acted upon for many years, Davidson persisted and in 1909 armed a Cadillac with a machine-gun. In 1910 he converted two more Cadillacs to balloon destroyers by fitting high-angle machine-guns. They were later given searchlights and radios and were successfully entered

Davidson's Cadillacs were a great improvement on the Duryea and steam cars. This 1911 version had a searchlight mounted alongside the Colt machine-gun.

Davidson's Cadillac armoured car of 1915. The driver's head was covered by a guard, with the Colt machine-gun behind a shield in the open fighting compartment. None of Davidson's designs was officially adopted by the US Army, which has never relied greatly on armoured cars.

in a gruelling cross-country run which resulted in an order from the Guatemalan Army for four more. Despite a lack of official encouragement, Davidson continued to convert Cadillacs and devised reconnaissance cars, a field kitchen and an ambulance. In 1915 he produced the United States' first armoured car, which had a box-shaped, open body with two Colt machine-guns covered by shields. The armoured Cadillac was never officially adopted by the US Army, but it

The 1906 Armstrong-Whitworth armoured car on trials in Newcastle, demonstrating the obstacle-crossing capability of its large wooden-spoked wheels. There were plans to fit a 1 pdr pom-pom next to the driver, but it could also be used as an artillery tractor.

ABOVE: *Isotta Fraschini were renowned for their powerful sports cars and even the 1911 armoured car which served in Libya could attain 37 mph (60 km/h) despite weighing 3 tons. Its body was 4 mm (0.16 inch) thick and steel discs covered the front wheels, which were fitted with wide flanges to prevent the car sinking in soft sand.*

BELOW: *One of the early Lancia IZ armoured cars with twin machine-gun turrets, seen shortly after completion at the Ansaldo works. The rails above the engine compartment were intended to cut through wire obstacles in the car's path. The Lancia, which weighed nearly 4 tons, had a 25/35 horsepower engine that gave it a top speed of 44 mph (70 km/h).*

The Italian Army used the 1917-model Lancia IZ for many years. It fought in the Civil War in Spain and was still in use during the Second World War. The armoured car had a high ground clearance and could cross rough terrain, but this Lancia seen in East Africa has smashed a front axle.

was used to train students at the North-western Military Academy into the 1920s.

In Britain the rejection of Simms's War Car initially discouraged further developments, but in 1906 an Ivel agricultural tractor was fitted with a simple armoured body for trials with the Royal Marines. In the same year the Newcastle firm of Sir W. G. Armstrong Whitworth manufactured an armoured body for a car designed by Walter Gordon Wilson. Wilson, who later partnered Sir William Tritton in designing the first tanks, had made a special study of transmissions and his Armstrong Whitworth car was the first armoured vehicle to have an epicyclic pre-selector gearbox. The engine was protected, but virtually the whole of the driver's body was exposed to enemy fire. There were plans to arm the car with a 1 pdr pom-pom but it could also be used as an artillery tractor. In 1913 Armstrong built an enclosed armoured car with a machine-gun mounted in a cylindrical turret for the Russian government, but no armoured vehicles were used by the British Army until the First World War.

Armoured cars were first used in a combat zone by the Italian Army, which sent a large motorised force to Libya when the Italo-Turkish War began in 1911. The trucks, mostly Fiats, were soon followed by an armoured car which had been donated by the Automobile Club of Milan. It was a 40 horsepower Isotta Fraschini, fully armoured, with one Maxim machine-gun in a rotating turret and another in the hull. Several Isotta Fraschinis were built and they arrived in Libya in 1912 together with a similar Fiat which had been armoured at Turin Arsenal. In the same year Bianchi built a 20/30 horsepower armoured car. The company developed similar vehicles after the start of the war in Europe, although the most important Italian armoured car of the First World War was the Lancia IZ, which entered production in 1915. The 4 ton vehicle was based on a 60 horsepower Lancia lorry chassis and armoured with 8 mm (0.31 inch) plate by the Genoese firm of Ansaldo-Fossatti. It was a conventional armoured car, although three machine-guns were mounted in a curious twin-tiered turret. In 1917, after thirty models had been completed, the upper turret was dropped from the design and 120 more Lancia-Ansaldos were built with the third machine-gun mounted in the rear of the hull. Each car carried fifteen thousand rounds of ammunition and twenty hand grenades and had a crew of six, comprising a commander, driver, mechanic and three gunners. The Lancia had a long career and was still used by the Italian Army in East Africa during the Second World War.

Belgian Army Minerva armoured cars at Houthem, near Ypres, in September 1917. They all have 8 mm machine-guns.

DEVELOPMENTS DURING THE FIRST WORLD WAR

In August 1914 no army used armoured cars in any quantity, but the outbreak of war accelerated production in nearly all the belligerent nations. Development followed similar lines in most countries and the first vehicles were relatively basic. They were mostly large touring cars or lorries fitted with improvised armoured bodies and armed with machine-guns. Later, standardised patterns of armour were devised but there were no specially built chassis. Instead, commercial vehicles were strengthened and adapted to meet the requirements of active service.

BELGIUM

The Belgians were the first to make widespread offensive use of motor cars, using them in the opening weeks of the war to carry sharpshooters in raids on the German Army. In August 1914 Lieutenant Charles Henkart, a keen motorist, allowed his two Minerva tourers to be armoured at the Cockerill Works in

Hoboken and with a group of aristocratic companions used them on scouting and intelligence-gathering missions. Henkart and Prince Baudouin were killed in an ambush on 6th September 1914, but by then a standard armoured body for the Minerva was already in production. It was based on the chassis of a 38 horse-power touring car, with a Knight-type four-cylinder double-sleeve valve engine that had already proved successful in racing. The car had an open body, 4 mm (0.16 inch) thick, which was fitted at Minerva's Antwerp factory. It was armed with an 8 mm Hotchkiss machine-gun protected by a shield, although some cars had 37 mm cannons. The Minerva weighed 4 tons and had a top speed of about 25 mph (40 km/h). The Kellner Works at Billancourt in France also armoured several Mors tourers and two Peugeots for the Belgian Army.

Although Minervas were still used in the 1930s the deaths of Henkart and

Prince Baudouin in an open-topped vehicle showed the inadequacies of the early armoured cars and prompted SAVA to build an enclosed body on a sporting chassis. The machine-gun armament was in a dome-shaped turret, open at the rear, which was later used on some Minervas.

GREAT BRITAIN

As the Belgian Army introduced the first armoured Mors and Minervas, British forces nearby were also operating in armoured cars. The development of the British vehicles, however, was pioneered not by the Army but by the Royal Naval Air Service (RNAS), which sent a squadron to France at the end of August 1914 to counter the threat of German Zeppelin attacks. The RNAS unit used a fleet of vehicles to transport ground crews, but the commanding officer, Charles Samson, realised that they could also be used for scouting and airfield defence. Like the Belgians, Commander Samson began by arming touring cars with machine-guns. He fitted a Maxim to a 45/50 horsepower Mercedes and, with a Rolls-Royce carrying riflemen, used it to ambush a German car near Cassel on 4th September 1914. Samson appreciated that protection for the engine and crew was essential and so, working to designs

prepared by his brother Felix, the Dunkirk shipbuilding firm of Forges et Chantiers de France armoured the Rolls-Royce, the Mercedes and some other cars. The 'armour' was boiler plate which could resist bullets fired only from ranges of over 500 yards (457 metres). The engines and gunners were partly shielded but the cars were still open as they could not support more armour without greater modification.

Felix Samson next designed new bodies for the AEC B-Type buses which the Royal Marines used as personnel carriers. These were also armoured in Dunkirk. Although they were mechanically reliable, the AECs were not fast enough to keep up with the cars and were rarely used in action. One B-Type chassis, however, served as a platform for a 3 pdr gun and together with an armoured Mercedes truck was used until the end of November.

The success of Samson's cars led the Admiralty Air Department to design bodies for a variety of chassis, mainly Rolls-Royces, Talbots and Wolseleys. Each car had the engine and bodywork completely covered in 8 mm (0.31 inch) plate, with a head guard over the driver's position. To take the extra weight of armour, the cars had twin rear wheels but the Wolseleys' axles were still not strong

Wolseleys with the first Admiralty pattern of armour leading a column through Belgium in October 1917.

A heavily laden Rolls-Royce of 10th (RN) Armoured Motor Battery at Voi in British East Africa. The durable armoured car was known as the 'kifaru' — rhinoceros — by the native askaris.

enough and most were converted to tenders after a short time. The majority of these 'First Admiralty Pattern' cars were Talbots with four-cylinder 25/50 horsepower engines. They were similar to the other cars but had large armoured plates over the radiators. These early Wolseleys, Talbots and Rolls-Royces were not popular with the RNAS because the machine-gun crews were left completely exposed from the waist up, so at least six of the Talbots were given extra side armour and more machine-guns.

Following criticism of the open-topped

The Sizaire-Berwick 'Wind Waggon' was an experimental armoured car built by the RNAS in 1915 and designed to cross soft sand. It was powered by a 110 horsepower Sunbeam aero engine which left no room for a turret, so its machine-gun was mounted next to the driver. The 'Wind Waggon' was tested in Britain but never saw action.

14

A Seabrook of C Section, Number 5 Squadron, with two of the seven crew manning the 3 pdr. The sides dropped to form a platform for the main armament and four machine-guns. All RNAS armoured car crews were enlisted as Petty Officers.

cars, the Admiralty Air Department formed a committee to design a turreted vehicle based on the Rolls-Royce, the toughest and most reliable car available. All Rolls-Royce chassis still under construction or awaiting bodywork were requisitioned and the first Admiralty turreted cars were ready in December 1914. The design was simple. The car had a central fighting compartment with a revolving turret on top. The driver sat on the floor while the two crewmen stood and worked the machine-gun, although occasionally the Rolls-Royce went into action with a two-man crew. Then the driver helped to feed ammunition into the machine-gun with one hand and steered with the other. The turret was supported on ball bearings and the gunner traversed it by leaning against the machine-gun mounting.

The Rolls-Royce was one of the most advanced vehicles of its day and had full pressure lubrication, electric trembler coil starting and an internal lighting system. However, it exhibited many of the characteristics of the early armoured cars. The six-cylinder 40/50 horsepower engine had a maximum output of 80 horsepower and gave the 3.5 ton vehicle a top speed of 50 mph (80 km/h) on good roads. The main fuel tanks were on the

The interior of the 1914-pattern turreted Rolls-Royce. The driver sat on the floor with the gunner and commander crouched alongside, all peering through narrow vision slits. The controls on the steering wheel were for adjusting the ignition and carburettor jet, with the handbrake and gear lever on the driver's right.

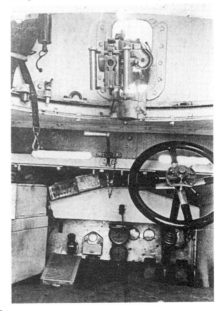

15

rear stowage platform and there was a 6 gallon (27 litre) gravity-feed petrol tank in the dashboard, which obviously increased the risk of fire. The car's range was limited by a fuel consumption rate of 8 mpg (2.8 km/l). It was driven through its rear wheels only and there were no front brakes, so stopping was not always easy. The wire-spoked wheels usually had narrow, high-pressure pneumatic tyres and spares were always carried because of the frequent punctures. Some cars had semi-solid 'Rubberine' tyres but these did not retain their shape and gave a very rough ride if a car stood still for too long.

In November 1914 Samson's original squadrons were organised into the Royal Naval Armoured Car Division (RNACD). Within four months there were fifteen squadrons, six equipped with machine-gun armed motorcycles and six with Rolls-Royces. Three others had a new type of armoured car, the Lanchester, developed from a 38 horsepower tourer. The body was almost identical to the Rolls-Royce pattern except that the Lanchester engine was mounted alongside the driving seat, thus allowing the frontal armour to be sloped for improved protection. The car was armed with a Vickers machine-gun and an extra Lewis gun, carried in the crew compartment. Complete with armour, it weighed over 4 tons and carried a crew of four.

The Lanchester and Rolls-Royce were the only turreted armoured cars used in any quantity by the RNAS, although similar vehicles were built on Talbot and Delaunay-Belville chassis. The Talbots were converted from the same 25/50 horsepower chassis as the earlier cars, but only three were built because they were unreliable. Delaunay-Belville, however, had a reputation which rivalled that of Rolls-Royce and three of the French-built cars were armoured and given simple cylindrical turrets. Despite their high quality, they were not put into production, although the body of one was later fitted to a Killen-Strait tractor during the experiments that led to the development of the first tank.

The success of Samson's 3 pdr Mercedes and AEC trucks led to orders for further well armed vehicles to support the machine-guns of the lighter cars. The German-built Mercedes were obviously in short supply and there were no suitable British petrol-engined lorries, so the RNAS adopted American Seabrooks, produced by the Standard Motor Truck Corporation of Detroit. The Seabrook

Wolseley Motors Limited built sixteen anti-aircraft lorries for the Royal Marine Artillery, using 5 ton Pierce Arrow lorry chassis imported from the United States. The four batteries they equipped shot down about twenty aeroplanes with their 2 pdr pom-poms.

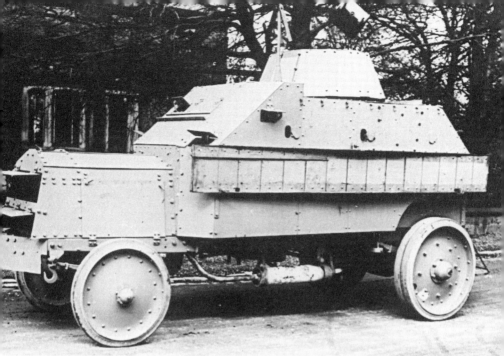

ABOVE: *One of the Leylands of the 1st Armoured Motor Battery, Machine Gun Corps, at Leyland Motors in 1915. It has a searchlight on the turret and unditching beams stowed on the sides. In East Africa the Leylands were stripped of some of their armour in an attempt to reduce weight, but they were still too heavy and were eventually sent to Egypt for use in security operations.*

BELOW: *Colonel T. E. Lawrence — 'Lawrence of Arabia' — had a variety of motor vehicles under his command in Palestine, but he valued the Rolls-Royces above all. They included armoured cars, and tenders like this one which transported men and equipment.*

was chain-driven with a four-cylinder 32 horsepower Continental engine. Its 3 pdr gun was mounted on a turntable and the 8 mm (0.31 inch) thick sides folded down to provide a gun platform for the five-man crew. The first Seabrooks were delivered in February 1915 and three were issued to each RNAS squadron. They were used for infantry support and attacks on strongpoints but their low speed and lack of manoeuvrability prevented them from working with the light armoured cars, so in May 1915 they were formed into separate heavy squadrons.

The Seabrooks stationed in England served as anti-aircraft lorries, touring the east coast as defence against raiding Zeppelins. In France and Belgium the Royal Marine Artillery used Pierce Arrow anti-aircraft lorries. They each had a 2 pdr, capable of firing four rounds per minute, mounted in an open-topped armoured compartment. The Pierce Arrow batteries were in action until 1917, while sixteen similar chain-driven Peerless vehicles were sold to the Russian government in 1916.

As trench fighting set in, the role of the armoured cars became increasingly restricted and they were mainly confined to liaison work. During 1915 and 1916, therefore, the RNAS were sent to theatres of war where they could have greater effect. Three squadrons were shipped to the Dardanelles in the spring of 1915 but found that conditions were similar to those in France, so the crews spent most of their time as infantrymen. In July 1915 the armoured cars took part in a frontal assault on the Turkish trenches but most were abandoned after failing to cross No Man's Land.

Number 1 Squadron RNAS arrived in German South-West Africa (Namibia) in April 1915 and in their first action five cars repulsed a strong attack by German infantry. The Rolls-Royces withstood the punishing conditions well, although they had frequent punctures and could not cross the roughest terrain. When the fighting moved into the almost impassable jungles of the Cameroons the cars were withdrawn and sent to East Africa. They proved so successful that three extra 'batteries' of armoured cars, under Army control, were sent to join them.

One of the batteries was a privately raised force with four Leyland armoured cars. Based on 3 ton, 30/40 horsepower trucks, these had 5 mm (0.20 inch) armour plate and two machine-guns, one in a turret, the other in the hull. Each had a six-man crew that included two drivers because there was an extra steering position for reversing. Although unditching boards were carried to help the Leylands cross muddy ground, the cars were far too heavy to cope with the appalling African roads during the rainy season. The Rolls-Royces had a much greater influence on the campaign, in which crews had to endure intense heat and disease in addition to enemy fire.

In Egypt and Libya, three Rolls-Royce batteries fought against the Turkish-backed Senussi sect. As the cars could not cross the stony areas of desert or patrol during the wet season, a Light Car Corps was formed. The Corps had un-armoured Model T Fords armed with Lewis guns. Once they had proved their value in the Western Desert they were transferred to more active fronts and in the final two years of the war fought in Palestine and Syria and with T. E. Lawrence's Hejaz Armoured Car Battery. The units were usually employed on reconnaissance duties attached to cavalry divisions but often operated far in advance of the mounted troops. They were also used for escort duties and rescuing downed pilots.

The expansion of the RNACD continued until the summer of 1915, by which time there were twenty active squadrons. Because the increasing involvement of the RNAS in land operations created divisions within both the Admiralty and the War Office, in September 1915 the RNACD was disbanded and the Army officially took over operations. The transfer took time, however, and aroused such opposition that some units remained under naval control until the end of the war.

In anticipation of the hand-over, the War Office sponsored several experimental armoured car designs. The first was based on a B-Type bus chassis and was similar to Felix Samson's earlier personnel carrier. It had an armoured driver's cab, but the rear compartment

ABOVE: *The tiny Autocarrier was totally unsuited for conversion to an armoured vehicle but the War Office built one on the 10 horsepower chassis and tested it at Aldershot in 1915. With only a 1.5 litre engine it could not match the performance of the larger RNAS cars, so only the prototype was completed.*

BELOW: *The first of the Westmorland and Cumberland Yeomanry's 25 horsepower Isotta Fraschinis designed by C. W. Lowther, an officer in the regiment. Some of the yeomanry cars were at least as good as the War Office vehicles but they were never put into production.*

Lanchesters of the Russian Armoured Car Division in Asia Minor. Similar vehicles were used by the Russian Army, but Locker-Lampson preferred the Rolls-Royce. Despite repeated appeals for Rolls-Royce armoured cars, however, the Lanchester remained the most common RNAS car on the Eastern Front.

was open and the armour plate could not resist bullets fired from close range. After reports had highlighted the shortcomings of the RNAS B-Types used in France, the project was halted.

A much lighter vehicle, on a strengthened two-seater car chassis, was built by Autocarrier (AC) of Thames Ditton. Armour covered the engine and there was a circular compartment for the gunner and driver. War Office trials, however, showed that the AC was far inferior to the Admiralty cars and so, again, only a prototype was completed.

The War Office vehicles were relative failures but motorists in some volunteer and yeomanry regiments designed armoured cars that were used in training. In November 1914 Lieutenant (later Captain) C. W. Lowther, an officer in the Westmorland and Cumberland Yeomanry, devised a body for a 25 horsepower Isotta Fraschini which was armoured by Guy Lewin Limited. The crew compartment was armoured and there were heavy doors over the radiator. A month later the same bodybuilders built a second Isotta Fraschini armoured car with the body and engine completely covered. The front plate sloped dramatically and

A partially completed Pierce Arrow of the Russian Armoured Car Division at the armourers, W. G. Allen and Sons of Tipton. The wooden sides of the rear stowage platform were later reinforced with sheet metal. The 3 pdr was mounted in the large turret, but with 9 mm (0.35 inch) armour the car weighed 9 tons and could operate only on hard ground.

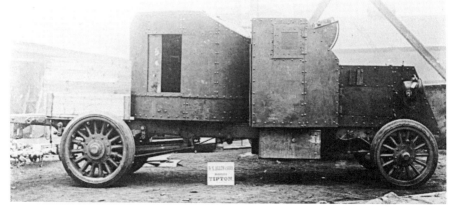

An RNAS armoured Model T Ford shortly after completion at W. G. Allen's Tipton yard. The body was designed by Chief Petty Officer Gutteridge, who served in the Russian Armoured Car Division. This one has a Stepney rim — a temporary cover — clamped to a front wheel because of a puncture.

the rear was also sharply angled, giving the car an unusual appearance. Other yeomanry armoured cars included a Rolls-Royce, two Wolseleys and a Talbot that, like the Isotta Fraschinis, never saw combat.

The yeomanry cars were never officially adopted by the Army, which relied on Admiralty vehicles to equip the new Armoured Motor Batteries, formed in 1915. The Royal Navy, however, still retained some armoured cars. Number 20 Squadron continued to test armoured vehicles, including the new tanks, while another force, under Commander Oliver Locker-Lampson MP, went east to assist the Russian Army. Known as the Russian Armoured Car Division, it consisted mainly of Lanchesters but was also equipped with a Rolls-Royce armoured car and several Seabrook and Pierce Arrow lorries. The Pierce Arrows were based on the anti-aircraft trucks used by the Royal Marines but had 3 pdr guns in heavy turrets mounted on turntables.

The Division was sent initially to Trans-Caucasia where it fought both the Turkish Army and Kurdish tribesmen. The Russians were impressed by a devastating armoured car attack on a Turkish-held village in August 1916, so the Division was transferred to the Rumanian front and reinforced with nine Model T Fords, chosen because of their good cross-country performance. The bodies were designed at the RNAS repair depot in Newport, Gwent. The rugged Fords had armoured cabs with Vickers machine-guns on their open rear decks. In 1917, however, the Russian Armoured Car Division was almost continually on the retreat. A disastrous offensive in Galicia followed the February Revolution and the RNAS sustained heavy losses fighting a rearguard action. The October Revolution brought an end to the Division's role with the Russian Army and when it left, early in 1918, the worn-out cars were left behind. Within a few months, however, the same RNAS

21

ABOVE: *'Lottchen' was used by a German Freikorps unit in 1919 but had originally been captured in Russia. The make of the chassis is not known but with its twin staggered turrets and 'wings' protecting the water-cooling jackets of the machine-guns the car closely resembles the Izhorskiy-Fiat.*

BELOW: *The massive Putilov-Garford was one of the most powerfully armed armoured cars of the First World War. One of the eight crewmen is leaning against the steel channels shielding the 76 mm gun, his arms around the co-axial Maxim machine-gun. Another crewman is standing beneath one of the sponson-mounted machine-guns.*

Heavy Povlavko-Jefferys on the Eastern Front. The turreted armoured car is a British-built Lanchester.

crews were back, supporting the White Russians and defending the Caucasian oilfields from Turkish attack.

RUSSIA

The British, French and Belgian armoured car forces that fought on the Eastern Front were heavily outnumbered by their Russian allies. The Russian Army had shown an early interest in armoured vehicles, partly because of their value in internal security operations, and formed an Automobile Corps in 1914. At the outbreak of war more armoured cars were used by the Russian Army than by any other. The first fifteen Russian armoured cars were built at the Russo-Balt factory in Riga in 1913 and fought near Lodz in the early months of the war. They were based on Type M lorries and were each armed with three machine-guns. Few of the early Russian vehicles were home-produced, however, and the majority were imported from Britain and France. They included Isotta Fraschini and Sheffield-Simplex armoured cars but they were not ideally suited to the conditions, so the largest Russian order went to the Austin Motor Company of Birmingham.

The first Austin armoured cars, built on 30 horsepower 'Colonial' chassis, were delivered in October 1914. They had twin machine-gun turrets, placed side by side, and solid, studded tyres for improved grip on the poor Russian roads. On arrival some of the cars were rebuilt and given thicker armour at the Putilov Works in Petrograd (now Leningrad) and the turrets were staggered to provide a better field of fire. Later models were given pneumatic tyres and dual rear wheels. Austin supplied about one hundred completed vehicles to the Russian Army, but Putilov also built their own versions on chassis shipped from Britain. These all had rear steering wheels for easier reversing, a modification later incorporated on all the Austins.

Although the Austin was the armoured car most frequently encountered in Russia, there were about thirty other types. In 1915, for example, Izhorskiy developed an armoured body for the Fiat 60 horsepower truck. Like the Austin, it had diagonally arranged twin turrets and, although smaller, still had a five-man crew. Putilov, the shipbuilding and armament firm, was the largest single armoured car manufacturer, and the in-

23

Peugeot armoured cars crewed by marines, at Magnicourte in May 1915.

fluence of naval engineers was evident in some of their heavy designs, such as the Putilov-Garford. This was based on an American lorry and armed with a 76 mm gun and machine-gun in a large rear turret, with two further machine-guns in sponsons on either side. With armour 9 mm (0.35 inch) thick, it weighed 11 tons so the 35 horsepower engine gave a top speed of only 12 mph (20 km/h). Despite a lack of mobility the Putilov-Garford had considerable firepower and was still used by the Red Army in the 1930s.

The Russian Army, like others, benefited from the ingenuity of experienced motorists. One of the most inventive was Staff Captain Mgebrov. His 18 horsepower Renault armoured car took advantage of the original vehicle's layout and had sharply sloped armour that ensured the crew's immunity from small arms fire. Although at 3.5 tons it was heavy, it was still produced after the Bolshevik Revolution. A similar Mgebrov-Benz was built only in small numbers after Mgebrov's death in action in 1916. Another officer, Staff Captain Povlavko, devised a heavily armoured car based on the American Jeffery Quad lorry. The turretless car weighed 8 tons and, despite armour

16 mm (0.63 inch) thick, had a top speed of 20 mph (32 km/h). Like the Austins, it had dual controls and, because its five-speed gearbox operated in either direction, a high-speed reverse. As the four-wheel-drive Quad could cross rougher terrain than most armoured cars the War Ministry ordered thirty Povlavko-Jefferys in 1916. The machine-gun armed cars were used to crush wire and assault enemy trenches on the south-western front. 'Heavies' were also built on Packard and Pierce Arrow lorries, but the severe Russian weather often prevented effective operations so the Army turned to vehicles with greater mobility. 'Half-tracks', with wheels on the front axle and tracks on the rear, were devised by Colonel Gulkievich and by the Tsar's chief automobile engineer, Adolphe Kegresse. After the October Revolution, Putilov converted Red Army Austins and Packards to half-tracks by fitting them with Kegresse or American-built tracks. They fought during the Civil War and in the harsh conditions were much better than conventional armoured cars.

FRANCE

The first French armoured units were

formed in August 1914 and touring cars were soon replaced by rudimentary armoured vehicles like the Peugeot. Renault, the largest single French automobile manufacturer, became involved in armoured car construction at an early stage. The company completed its first order for one hundred vehicles in November 1914 and these were in action a month later, manned by marines. The 18 horsepower cars, which were fitted with twin rear wheels and St Etienne machine-guns, had only minimal protection, so subsequent models were built using 5 mm (0.20 inch) plate. At first sloping armoured covers surrounded the engine until Renault introduced an armoured version of their famous bonnet and located the radiator grilles at the front of the crew compartment. They also produced an 'autocanon', based on the open-bodied armoured car, which was armed with a 37 mm gun.

Renault's venture into heavy armoured car production was less successful. The company built four 47 mm gun 'autocanons' based on 2.5 ton trucks, but they were very slow and were used only briefly as part of an anti-aircraft section which served near Dunkirk in June 1915.

Engineers and soldiers also devised armoured cars for the French Army and one, designed by Segur and Lorfeuvre,

was used for many years. The White armoured car was a conventional vehicle built on an imported American lorry chassis. The only unusual feature was that its 37 mm gun and machine-gun were mounted on opposite sides of the turret. Over two hundred Whites were built and when the original chassis wore out in the 1930s the armoured bodies were removed and fitted to French-built Lafflys.

UNITED STATES OF AMERICA

Although American chassis like the White were used as the basis of armoured cars in several countries, the United States' isolation from the European conflict until 1917 meant that few American armoured cars saw combat during the First World War. Nevertheless, several companies produced commercial designs, including Mack (The International Motor Company). In 1915 they began construction of three armoured cars in conjunction with White and Locomobile (Riker). Each of the companies provided its own chassis but the cars had identical hulls. The armour was sloped inwards, which complicated construction but improved protection. The open-topped vehicles, which each weighed 4 tons, were built in sections and could be converted into armoured trucks by removing the bodies. The Mack was armed with two Colt

Renault 'autocanons' passing a line of cavalry. The armoured car gradually took over the traditional cavalry role, although in most armies the conversion was not fully accomplished until the Second World War.

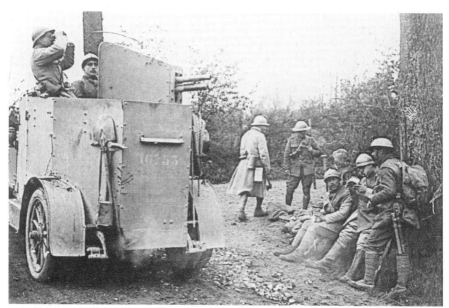

ABOVE: *French Army Renaults operating in support of British troops during the German attack on Meteren in April 1918. The 37 mm gun was covered by a shield, but the crews were still left exposed to enemy fire.*

LEFT CENTRE: *The Renault 47 mm 'autocanon' was designed for operations on the flat battlefields of northern France and could engage targets at long range. The heavy armour made the car so slow, however, that it was hardly ever used in combat.*

LEFT BELOW: *White armoured cars of the French Volunteer Company in Shanghai in July 1927. These have the solid tyres and wooden wheels of the original and machine-guns in the turret fronts.*

The 2 ton Mack truck chassis awaiting the fitting of the armoured body. Butt straps strengthen the angle-iron framework. The chain-driven truck had twin rear wheels, with solid rubber blocks for tyres.

The completed Mack armoured car. The specially hardened steel for the body was supplied by the Carnegie Steel Corporation and held in place by over six hundred bolts. The car had two Colt machine-guns and a 10 inch (25 cm) searchlight.

machine-guns, mounted on stands and covered by shields, and all the cars had loopholes for rifles. The three armoured cars were bought by wealthy citizens and donated to the 1st Armored Motor Battery of the New York National Guard, who used them in training and on recruiting campaigns. Mack claimed to be 'ready to build duplicates on short notice' but, although the cars patrolled the Mexican frontier in 1916, there were no new orders and the battery was disbanded a year later.

Tension on the southern border of the United States inspired as many American designs as the First World War. In 1916 White built a turreted armoured car which was produced in modified form for trials at Rock Island Arsenal and with the Ordnance Department. The Armored Motor Car Company of Detroit also built several vehicles, based on King Tourers, which resembled the RNAS cars. One

vehicle completed over 4000 miles (6437 km) of trial running under US Army and Marine supervision and modified Kings were used by the Marines in the 1920s. In 1917, however, the Allied Commission advised the United States against armoured car construction, so only the experimental vehicles sent to the Mexican border saw active service with the US Army between 1914 and 1918. Nevertheless, American armoured cars were used on European battlefields during the First World War.

CANADA
    In October 1914 the Canadian Army took delivery of twenty armoured machine-gun carriers built by the Autocar Company of Ardmore, Pennsylvania. They arrived in France in 1915 and were used there until the end of the war. A privately financed Canadian unit, the Eaton Motor Battery, also had forty

LEFT: *The Canadian Autocars were primarily intended as machine-gun carriers and in normal circumstances did not have to stand and fight. The fate of the crew of this knocked-out Autocar demonstrates the dangers faced in the open-topped, lightly armoured cars of the First World War.*

RIGHT: *A Jeffery Quad of 8th Armoured Car Company in India. The Jefferys were still in use in 1924, 'a grievous disappointment' to soldiers in the Royal Tank Corps who had expected to serve in Rolls-Royces. The poor quality armour did little for morale and there was a grave shortage of spares as the ship carrying parts had been torpedoed.*

LEFT: *An Indian-pattern armoured car built at the Lillooah railway workshops in 1915 and based on a Minerva tourer. The rounded projections in the hull sides allowed the gun crew to fire the Maxim from any position. Metal discs covered the wooden spokes of the front wheels. These were soon discarded, but the acetylene gas headlamps remained.*

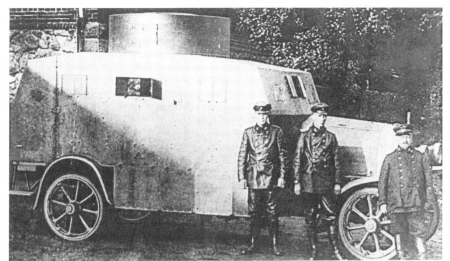

The 1915-model Ehrhardt, the prototype for the standard German armoured car of the First World War. The turret could not be traversed, so the car had ten alternative ports for Maxims. The pintle on the bonnet could be used to mount a flag or, if one of the crew was prepared to take a risk, an anti-aircraft gun.

armoured cars based on the Jeffery Quad chassis. They were assembled by the Canada Cycle and Motor Company Limited of Toronto and were developed from prototypes built at Jeffery's works in Kenosha, Wisconsin. The Jeffery Quad had a Vickers machine-gun in a large, centrally mounted turret and there were two sponsons with loopholes for pistols. The 40 horsepower Buda engine gave the car a nominal top speed of 20 mph (32 km/h) but parts usually fell off if the driver exceeded 10 mph (16 km/h). The four-wheel drive Quad had steering and brakes on all wheels, but its cross-country performance was restricted by its excessive weight and solid tyres. As the Jefferys were of no use on the Western Front, in 1917 they were given to the British government and sent to assist in security operations in India and Ireland.

INDIA

The Quads in India joined an odd assortment of vehicles that patrolled the cities and the troubled outposts along the North-West Frontier. The early Indian cars were armoured with boiler plate and armed with obsolete Maxim machine-guns. As the Indian Armoured Motor

Batteries expanded, the Railway Workshops in Lahore and Lillooah built standardised models on requisitioned cars using 6 mm (0.24 inch) plate shipped from Britain. A number were also built on Fiat lorries, with bodywork based on the War Office AEC design. The Indian cars were basic even by the standards of the first RNAS vehicles, but they were used throughout the war. In the inter-war years most of the British Army's armoured cars were based in India.

GERMANY

The German Army was slow to copy the Allied use of armoured cars and the first specialised vehicles of the war were not completed until 1916. The three experimental armoured cars were built by Büssing, Daimler and Ehrhardt, and all had four-wheel drive and duplicate rear steering. The Daimler carried a crew of eight or nine who manned three Maxim machine-guns which could be fired through loopholes in a fixed turret or from ports in the hull. The Ehrhardt was a similar, box-bodied vehicle, but had a cylindrical turret. These enormous armoured cars each weighed nearly 9 tons but could still attain 38 mph (60 km/h).

29

The sheer size of the German armoured cars is evident in this view of three of the experimental vehicles and their 29 crewmen. The heaviest, and largest, is the 90 horsepower Büssing and alongside is the 1915 prototype Ehrhardt. The furthest vehicle is a Daimler with a fixed cylindrical turret instead of the built-up superstructure of the original. It was one of three Daimler prototypes that did not reach the production stage.

The Büssing was even larger: it was 31 feet (9.4 metres) long and weighed 10 tons. It steered on all four wheels and could be driven in five speeds in either forward or reverse gear. Like the others, it was armed with three Maxims which could be mounted in the hull or fixed turret.

The three experimental German armoured cars fought on the Baltic, Verdun and Rumanian fronts during the course of 1916, and the Army received 32 more, all Ehrhardts, in 1917. The new Ehrhardts were similar to the 1915 prototype but were about a ton lighter despite added protection for the rear wheels and undersides. They also had rotating turrets and radios. The Ehrhardts, together with some captured vehicles, were formed into small units that fought mainly on the Eastern Front in the final year of the war. In the revolutionary period that followed the surrender, the surviving cars were used by police and paramilitary groups in Germany, and in 1919 Ehrhardt built twenty more for use as police cars.

ARMOURED CARS IN 1918

On the Western Front trench fighting prevented large scale armoured car operations for most of the war. The French Army vehicles were used mainly for escort and liaison duties, while British Light Armoured Batteries on the Somme and at Arras were hardly involved because of the poor conditions. In the final months of the war, however, armoured cars made a more effective contribution, although the presence of British vehicles in France was as much the result of accident as planning.

When the October Revolution halted exports to Russia, Austin armoured cars built for export were delivered to the British Army. They were virtually identical to the earlier vehicles but had dual rear wheels, a choice of 'Rubberine' or pneumatic tyres and slightly revised bodywork. Forty were sent to Mesopotamia (Iraq) in the spring and summer of 1918 and attached to 'Dunsterforce'. Crewed by men of the former Russian Armoured Car Division, they went north to Baku in the Caucasus where they safeguarded the exposed southern flank of the Russian front.

Part of the original Dunsterforce consignment was diverted to France where, because of tank shortages, it equipped the 17th Battalion of the Tank Corps. The Austins were identical to the earlier cars except for their Tank Corps standard .303 Hotchkiss machine-guns. The 17th Battalion co-operated briefly with the French Army and then took part in the decisive Amiens offensive which began on 8th August 1918. As the Allied armies advanced across France, the Austins and their French counterparts adopted the traditional cavalry role of scouting, defending the flanks and hampering the enemy retreat.

The fighting took a heavy toll on the Austins, which could not cross rough ground and were often disabled by broken axles. Observation from the cars was difficult because the driver and commander had to share the same vision slit, while showers of splash flew around inside if a car was hit, injuring the crews. The Austins usually worked in groups so that they could provide each other with covering fire, but they were highly vulnerable when faced with field guns and anti-tank rifles. Nevertheless, mobile workshop units managed to keep nearly all the cars in action and their presence on the front caused widespread panic in the German Army. At the end of the war the 17th Battalion led the Army of Occupation across the Rhine, an honour that recognised the armoured cars' impact in the final months of the conflict.

ABOVE LEFT: *Rolls-Royce armoured cars at Arras in April 1917. The chains on the rear wheels gave them better grip, but conditions on the Western Front favoured the tank, introduced in September 1916.*
ABOVE RIGHT: *An Austin armoured car of 17th Battalion, Tank Corps, advancing towards Warfusée on 8th August 1918.*
BELOW: *The 1919 Peerless was closely modelled on the Austin but was based on a larger, chain-driven truck chassis and so the body was slightly too small. First used in Ireland in 1920 it later equipped the fledgling Irish Army and some British territorial units and appeared on London streets during the General Strike of 1926.*

FURTHER READING

Champagne, Jacques P. *The Armoured Vehicles of the Belgian Army*. G. Everling, Arlon, Belgium, 1975.

Crow, Duncan (editor). *Armoured Fighting Vehicles of World War One*. Profile Publications, 1970.

Crow, Duncan, and Icks, Robert J. *Encyclopedia of Armoured Cars*. Barrie and Jenkins, 1976.

Fletcher, David. *War Cars — British Armoured Cars in the First World War*. Her Majesty's Stationery Office, 1987.

Forty, George. *A Photo History of Armoured Cars in Two World Wars*. Blandford Press, 1984.

Milsom, John F. *Russian Armoured Cars (to 1945)*. Profile Publications, 1973.

Operations of the 17th (Armoured Car) Tank Battalion During the Battle of 1918. Gale and Polden, 1920.

Perrett, Bryan, and Lord, Anthony. *The Czar's British Squadron*. William Kimber, 1981.

Robertson, Bruce. *Wheels of the RAF*. Patrick Stephens, 1983.

Rolls-Royce Armoured Cars and the Great Victory. Rolls-Royce, about 1919.

Samson, C. R. *Fights and Flights*. Ernest Benn, 1930.

Vanderveen, Bart. *Armour on Wheels*. Frederick Warne, 1976.

Vanderveen, Bart. *The Observer's Army Vehicles Directory to 1940*. Frederick Warne, 1974.

White, B. T. *British Tanks and Fighting Vehicles 1914-1945*. Ian Allan, 1970.

White, B. T. *Tanks and Other Armoured Fighting Vehicles, 1900 to 1918*. Blandford Press, 1970.

Zaloga, Steven J., and Grandsen, James. *Soviet Tanks and Combat Vehicles of World War Two*. Arms and Armour Press, 1984.

PLACES TO VISIT

GREAT BRITAIN

The Tank Museum, Bovington Camp, near Wareham, Dorset BH20 6JG. Telephone: Bindon Abbey (0929) 463953 or 462721 extension 329 or 463. There are no armoured cars built before the end of the First World War in Britain but the Tank Museum's collection includes a 1920-pattern Rolls-Royce (see cover) and a 1919 Peerless.

CANADA

Canadian War Museum, National Museum of Man, 330 Sussex Drive, Ottawa, Ontario.

IRELAND

Cavalry Barracks, The Curragh, Kildare. The Irish Army has a 1920 pattern Rolls-Royce, 'Slievenamon', preserved here.

UNITED STATES OF AMERICA

Museum of Science and Industry, 57th Street and South Lake Shore Drive, Jackson Park, Chicago, Illinois 60637. Contains Davidson's No. 2 steam car of 1902.

Patton Museum of Cavalry and Armor, Keyes Park, Fort Knox, Kentucky 40121.

US Army Ordnance Museum, US Army Ordnance Center and School, Aberdeen Proving Ground, Maryland 21040. The collection includes a Model E King and the Rock Island Arsenal White of 1916.

UNION OF SOVIET SOCIALIST REPUBLICS

Historical Artillery Museum of the Soviet Army, Lenin's Park 7, Leningrad.